EXPLORING THE ELUSIVE ART OF DUSTY SPRINGFIELD

CATHERINE J BELL

ISBN 978-1-911079-36-1

Acorn Independent Press

Quotes

Text

A Medley

Listen to Dusty Springfield!

Which Dusty ?

'Melancholy is a fearful gift, What is it but the telescope of truth ?'

Byron

'In the artist of all kinds I think one can detect an inherent dilemma, which belongs to the co-existence of two trends: the urgent need to communicate and the still more urgent need not to be found.'

D. Winnicott

‘Only music mattered to Dusty, and nothing else, not even people, ever came close.’

Dionne Warwick

'It's only a pop song, Dusty.'

Neil Tennant

'She was a fool to herself, that girl.'

Petula Clark

1

Mary Isobel Catherine Bernadette O'Brien was born in West Hampstead, London, in 1939, and grew up in Ealing. She died at her home in Henley-on-Thames, Oxfordshire, in April 1999.

She spent her public life as a singer called Dusty Springfield – the 'Dusty' she often claimed came from her mother's nickname for her but it's more likely she chose it herself because the two names, coming together serendipitously, sounded right.

Like her best music it was right and somehow inevitable.

2

A while ago, if you looked up a few of Dusty's obituaries, to get a sense of how she was seen in 1999, long past the years of her fame, you could have found in the *Daily Mail's'* online archive a tribute headed: ***'the voice that haunted a generation',*** an odd and perhaps perplexing reference for those who knew nothing about her career or her music.

And then, for reasons unknown, this adjective was later replaced by one which seems less bothersome, less retrospectively disturbing, more purely musical, happier, gaily nostalgic: ***'the voice that entranced a generation'***.

Most popular singers, successful ones, display a soothing sameness, the ability to engage you now with what has gone before – the sheer familiarity draws in your ear, perks up the response, stimulates associations, you know what to expect.

Dusty's music didn't work like that.

She both haunts and entrances, engages, alienates and sometimes just lets you down.

She sang pop songs in all their simplicity. But 'simple', she was not.

She resists understanding through the stories of pop mythology; she's indecipherable.

3

Many thousands of words have been written and several books have been filled with information and opinions about Dusty, while she was alive and then, more provocatively, after her death. Her recorded songs have been analysed and various roles considered for her as an 'icon' of the sixties and as a cultural icon at other times and in other ways. These accumulated perspectives depend largely on knowledge of her life in a social context, on her appearance, her sexuality, her promotions, if not appropriations, of the style and rhythms of American 'black' music, and ultimately her sound – in the context of which those pop tracks she laboured over so meticulously at Philips often seem at a distance of years only part of it all, a sidebar if you like, to discussions of her enduring appeal.

Her view of herself, revealed to others in interviews and various publicity paragraphs in the music press, is similarly complex and as often contradictory; she talked publicly to many people over her lifetime but rarely told a fraction of the truth to anyone. Along with other fabulists in the world of art she invented, fibbed a bit, but wasn't deceitful, not in a moral way. Every time she opened her mouth, in speech or in song, she discovered and kept finding different ways of describing and expressing herself, never lastingly content with any of them.

4

Who is Dusty, in the sixties ?

She's the girl who left the Springfields trio and then, in her midtwenties, went out on her own and wanted, needed the chart hits and press in Melody Maker and the NME – so she did some good danceable stuff for Philips, a bit over-busy to hear now and not songs which have endured.

Then, she's the interpreter of standards which fit oddly into her Top 40ish repertoire; the performer of idiosyncratic and rarely played B sides; the promoter of Motown music - the shuffling of categories which she tasted, inhabited so briefly and then abandoned so suddenly that her existing in them at all can only be interpreted as an expression of extreme restlessness, a psychological state bordering on attention deficit

Her drifting across boundaries, her indifference to the creation of a predictable and constant style also, exceptionally, allowed her to explore and express the interaction, the clash, between words, melody and meaning in different modes – whether conscious or not, and perhaps it wasn't, just instinct,

And of course her instincts, for newness and the adoption of different musical mannerisms, as easy to assume as a hairstyle or a fashion in clothes, resulted sometimes in commercial failure: the songs were sublime but only fans bought them.

5

So we trace Dusty's uncoordinated progress along the path of pop music – her choice of songs, which often seems haphazard – just what interested her from moment to moment – and results in a kind of musical solipsism, and an uncertain ear for popular taste, when left to herself, and therefore what was 'commercial' and ultimately a detachment from the popular culture within which she existed as a singer, and which, otherwise, would have defined her.

This fragmentation, the following of different musical trails which qualifies her status as 'legend' (for a 'legend' should be above all consistent) may be simply no more than that deficiency in attention - Dusty bored quickly – but then more ambitious, as a constant curiosity about the essential nature of what she sang and the search for a musical statement, a conclusion, she never found.

6

And then there's the puzzle about her status as a notable British pop singer – as an often recalled and referenced and frequently 'rediscovered' name whose ultimate reputation nevertheless seems to belong with those common to all arts who are more revered than listened to, looked at or read.

Her post-mortem life is immanent and ubiquitous – around us and often unidentified, on movie soundtracks, commercials – a hermetic presence. Yet in pop histories often 'marginal' or even 'absent'. Or qualified – she must be *'white-female-British-soul'*.

And after Dusty died, in biographical books and other pieces the lived reality and the irrelevantly hagiographical became conflicting stories where often the music is trivialised, dismissed or just unheard.

7

Dusty was a *pop singer* – that's what she did, that's who she was. In an era of cultural multitasking she didn't write songs, not really, she didn't act,(she was hopelessly stiff), she didn't make movies and in a time of turbulent politics and social movements she took no public stance and didn't seem very interested in the activities of a wider world.

Her own world, which she knew, was her music, her originality the unique and inimitable timbre of her voice, her extraordinarily apt musical phrasing and her distinctly different readings of an idiosyncratic choice of other people's compositions.

8

Dusty didn't write songs, as many of her contemporaries did, or pretended to, because she knew she had nothing to say which couldn't be conveyed through using her voice simply as an instrument.

She was bright enough, and maybe humble enough, to understand that she stood for no particular philosophy of life, had no message – that she was in no way exceptional except as an interpretative singer, a performer almost of a tradition of *lieder* in pop and to wander away from that category was a risk not worth taking.

9

The classic form of the pop song, the approximately 3 minute side of a 45rpm disc, was the medium which developed her and held her; it was her upbringing, eclectic sometimes in expression but elemental.

Dusty was constantly open to musical influences and borrowed a few but ultimately viewed them all through the same 45rpm prism.

10

The listener, coming across Dusty not as an historical contemporary but as a figure in the pop lexicon, will not hear constants, not a smooth segue from one version or another of the same catalogue, but the mapping of a career where her presence as a significant singer was brief and her recordings so lacking in any clear link in style or 'narrative' or similarity of theme that it's tempting to describe what happens as just brilliant pieces – and no actual development.

In the often postulated philosophical/psychological dichotomy of the 'narrative' versus the 'episodic' way of living a life Dusty can be located, and would possibly, had she considered it, located herself, firmly in the episodic.

It's surely as 'valid' as a narrative form – just a little harder to follow.

11

Looking back on the era which defined her, she's there with Cilla and Sandie and Lulu and Petula but she was not often seen with them, in no sense were they a group – and Petula met her only twice during the shared decade of their careers.

Dusty was also the first one to die.

For consciousness, or self-consciousness of those days you can look through *Goodbye Baby and Amen – A Saraband for the Sixties,* published in 1969 when that decade was hardly over , and you'll find no trace of Dusty, no bouffant blonde who was after all 30 when David Bailey shot those iconic faces and Peter Evans penned the text explaining our time to our time's prescient close.

It's not Dusty there, it's Lulu occupying a double page spread – the *virgin pop queen* – singing prettily, lustily, married to Maurice Gibb and lacking a secret life.

Perhaps Bailey and Evans might not have considered Dusty at all, not by 1969, not in the *narrative* any longer, and not representative or explicable as a performer who had been, during the sixties, seldom out of the pop limelight and yet the most enigmatic, the least revealing of herself as a star, as a public character.

And her records – *you couldn't write on them.*

12

Bailey may have overlooked Dusty but she herself never hid from the camera; a bit narcissistic, like most performers, she was aware of pictures and their place in the public's perception of her. She manicured and manipulated an image, but as often as the camera saw her one way she saw herself in another. So she was suspicious and a bit paranoid and scrutinised contact sheets with infinite care. She might have suspected the most unflattering photos (she could look quite different from different angles – those were the planes of her face) showed her the way she feared to be portrayed – not so much unattractive, but 'ordinary' – available to all.

And then the makeup she plastered on, a maquillage derived from the Queen Alexandra school of beauty, wasn't unusual for girls in the sixties, but was for Dusty a contemporary mode which allowed her to fit the fashion and hide at the same time.

Early on she became blonde – a blonde her green eyes belied, her natural hair was reddish, auburn, good Celtic colouring, but then *blondes have more fun.*

Her green eyes were Dusty's most distinctive feature; she knew that and her makeup drew attention to them.

'Her unfathomable eyes' – how Carol Pope, writing about Dusty many years later, described them.

So much unknowable about her.

In photos, for publicity and then more casually, her eyes can appear detached from her expression – unnervingly percipient and at other times just a bit blank and tired.

Press the shutter – I've posed enough and I've seen it all before.

13

She could also appear much younger than she was at the time, and then, with a shift in perspective, much older.

In later years there were photographs taken of Dusty and used to promote a certain effect where she looks drained and wasted, posing to prefigure her own 'legend' and superimposed on and contradicting, without her permission of course because by this time she was already dead, existing pictures displaying the more or less happiness and the great achievement of her youth and prime.

14

In her 'prime' (and how often do we come back to that word, so short was the span of fame in her timeline) her voice could be described, unmusically, as a lightly hoarse soprano, with a good range, and a 'rasp' employed sometimes in a masterly way to create unexpected emotion and to connect phrases. That this habit may also have led to destructive effects on her vocal cords may not have occurred to her or bothered her at the time.

'I abused my voice in the sixties', she said long after the sixties were gone. She meant her audience, begging for the famous hits, the arias, the ones you could sing along to and wait for the dramatic moments when she became as close as she ever needed to be to her fans.

At these moments she wasn't able to say no.

She wasn't able to say *'You Don't Have To Say You Love Me'* was the one song she shouldn't sing live any more.

Even when things were going wrong for her she was rarely able to say no.

15

Dusty sometimes sang, although she didn't appear to speak, with a lisp, a sibilance which in early days shows itself, on and off, as a slight thickness in articulation – often a bit charming, adding an unusual vocal nuance and colour to a song – but by the end of the sixties had developed into a characteristic which intruded itself into her music. Once you hear it you can't not hear it.

Joe

You've Got a Friend

One can only guess at which particular stresses or strains brought out this impediment in her voice.

16

What binds Dusty of The Springfields to the single Dusty of her nascent Top 40 career and then the splitting off into all those other lyrical forms and sets her that much apart from those other girl singers is something she did nothing more to earn than to be actually born with – the distinctive vocal timbre carrying with it a weight of knowing sadness, the soft and regretful edge through the frivolous and determinedly playful world of the evolving sixties pop song.

Was she aware of this gift of hers ? That the 'telescope of truth' which hangs inside her recorded voice is the constant in almost all her recorded music – it is the fluttering of a few pages from *The Anatomy of Melancholy*.

Those early hits, the superficially frisky songs are just the prelude to a threnody – what the promise seemed to be and then – what can and will go wrong.

Dusty's voice is not just a 'pop' voice and neither is it 'in the moment' for memoirists of cultural history – it's a perseverant counterpoint – the paying off of the sixties.

17

For example – listening to a compilation you could be surprised, taken aback, to come across, mixed with the raucousness, an unexpected sweetness in her voice, mixed with the melancholy strain that could isolate phrases in an otherwise mediocre track and find there a reason for listening to Dusty at all.

Time After Time

This is a musical moment which presages an eventual 'tragedy' if that word can be used to shadow the coming personal fall from grace and reaches out, as with all good artists, every hearers', readers', viewers' sadness.

It's there – born not so much from experience as from instinctive knowledge of how to use the vocal instrument and it's the theme running through song after song.

18

Dusty said once: 'Lyrics mean very little to me. I don't pay attention to lyrics until they're over'.

She just didn't seem interested in words, not *per se*; she often confused lyrics and had trouble remembering them.

So she didn't belong to that style of pop singing where words were fondled, their meaning dwelt on – if they had any. She recognised no doubt the inanity of most pop songs, taken as a serious commentary on life and things in life.

Instead she slipped over words, elided them, swallowed syllables, took them in with a breath and then lost them somewhere, or just ignored them, hurrying on to the next note.

It was the note, not the word. The sound, not the sense.

She might have been a bit dyslexic – or if not that, then so alive to the melody, so aware of the way her phrasing flowed over and around words, and so clear about the sense her timbre gave to the musical outcome, the finished product – well, the words didn't matter much did they ?

19

In The Land of Make Believe : As perfect a track as you could ever hear and but it's not the meaning of the words you're listening to – it's pure voice.

The song 'means' nothing – you can hear it in the background and miss the lyrics entirely and you've missed nothing – it's an instrumental.

Dusty sings in her upper range, her 'head' voice where words aren't always so clear and lyrical sense is reduced to pure sound, where melody, privileged over meaning, pushes literal meaning aside.

And it's absolutely unpretentious.

It's Over

Dusty covered this song by Jimmie Rodgers but she doesn't follow the original lyrics Rodgers wrote – and her version, although musically consistent, doesn't make much sense.

Of course she may not have ever seen the lyrics written down, she had a habit of foraging among tapes and acetates and picking out whatever appealed to her. Or she may have heard it on the radio and if she did see or hear the original, which was never a hit song, she might have liked the melody but considered the whole thing a bit word cluttered.

So she just cut out the clutter.

‘Copyright’ would not have bothered her. She could do what she liked. And the track was never released in her lifetime so no one noticed.

It’s one of Dusty’s ‘lost songs’ – and as fresh and clear to us now as it must have been on that spring day in 1968 when she went to Philips studios in Stanhope Place to record it. It’s a lovely song – her voice is at its peak, confidently moving through the endless musical phrases until the high notes finish, and the rasp is perfectly placed.

And then the tape, Vocal Take 7, was competed and left in the vaults until 32 years later when the track was discovered, put on a compilation and its way made out into the world.

20

Ideally Dusty might have wanted to create *songs without words.*

But that option was obviously not available to her as a more or less middle-of-the-road pop singer.

21

When she's not doing an 'aria' (those three minute operatic pop imitations) Dusty's songs are best ended on a fade – a conclusion for the recording studio only.

Otherwise there's sometimes a bit of gratuitous theatricality – a 'made' performance done for effect and she's not always good there. It all sounds a bit false and her best songs weren't really about that.

Goin' Back

On the fade you can sense where she knows she's not being 'heard' – that is there is no climax written for her and the machine would simply record the freedom she has to sing off for a few seconds into a kind of vocal play.

22

Dusty's backing singers were the handmaidens of her recording art.

They were sometimes friends, sometimes good session singers – a variable lineup over the years producing a chirpy girly sound as a counter to her own vocal maturity and which brings that quality forward in the mix.

She can appear, musically, the only grown-up voice around on the track.

Sometimes there's the basic call and response; on other songs the backing is wallpaper against which she can rise with the chorus and then cut through with a clean clear slice.

Don't Say it Baby

That's How Heartaches are Made

Take Me for a While

I'm Gonna Leave You

And sundry others.

There's a suggestion of the unconscious acting out of twin aspects of herself – an internal cohabitation – for her personality remained in many ways childish but what was sent out to the listening public, through the music she recorded and mainly chose herself, was a sensibility very different.

23

Dusty once said: 'people ask me who I think I sound like.'

Vicki Wickham said: 'if you're British you can't be authentic'. She meant 'authentic' as in the replication of blues and soul where the authenticity had to be imported.

But Dusty, paradoxically, invented a way of being authentic yet not really moving far from her middleclass English background.

Through the flexibility of her repertoire she assumed different vocal roles and at the same time held on to a resonance all her own.

There were vowel sounds which suited her voice and some of those were strongly present in songs she borrowed from the black tradition. She stretches out the acoustic components of words and alights on notes she acrobatically incorporates into the lyric stream.

24

Her voice is very often marked by a quality of 'coldness' and 'distance', as though she's standing back from the performance.

Her voice is 'cold' because it doesn't convey the quality of emotional warmth through a direct auditory mode. The feeling comes through the creation of distance.

And the distance which came naturally to her, through her voice, left her free to convey feeling in the aesthetic sense – and that works because the emotion you experience as a response to music is not the emotion which you know and understand in real life.

So she's not obviously an intimate singer, although sometimes she can assume that role through technical closeness created by space around the microphone. Good pop singers have always done that.

Second Time Around

A standard which veers strangely from the heroic to the *come hither*.

The mechanical aspect of recording closeness was something she knew very well although in real life closeness was always a problem for her.

25

Sometimes Dusty sang lyrics as though the English language contained no prepositions or pronouns – she jumps over these short words to give herself time for the vowels. Perhaps that's one of the secrets of her phrasing.

26

When Dusty elongates the open vowel sounds she also frequently slurs syllables, foregrounding her timbre and creating the floating, 'drifting' quality which was often noted and was, of course, often envied but never copied because no other singer could ever sound like her, not ever.

Far Away Places – 'callin' – she loved what that sound conveyed: plangent, flying off somewhere, and she used it again and again.

27

She had a hard edge to her voice as well – it's unexpected and the hardness can be cutting – she used it for contrast, clarity and surprise.

Take Me for a While

She can move in one track between robustness and frailty. In her prime she could switch this aspect on and off.

In later years the hardness softened and the frailty was genuine and of course couldn't be switched off.

28

In her music, if not in her actual practical day to day life, she was a calculating person and extremely intelligent – different musical techniques were artfully employed and taken for granted.

But improvisation, a feature of some of the American music she much admired, was not in her register.

Improvisation probably threatened *loss of control.*

The way Dusty used her voice needed to be structured and enclosed and this is why she was generally meticulous about her arrangements and her recording environment.

29

Dusty was notionally Irish (she sang Irish songs in live performance but never recorded any) and raised as a Catholic in the old tradition and she would have grown up as a girl and young woman hearing the precise tones and musical patterns of that liturgy.

She might have absorbed, perhaps in a subconscious way, and later applied, the qualities of ‘precision and restraint’ recognised by music critics later in her career.

(when Dusty was once asked about her church going she admitted she’d abandoned confession and other rituals ‘sometime in the sixties’ and would return to the faith of her youth only when the Latin Mass returned)

30

And when you consider the 'restraint', the 'containment' and how Dusty encountered and then reproduced emotion in music, the sense sometimes that she wasn't giving enough of herself directly, you have to take into account something she knew by instinct – that 'emotion' is best conveyed when it is not forced and her cool and controlled delivery evokes a response which isn't tangled and confused by passing joy or sadness.

It's Over

She once said she tried, when young, to put in more 'feeling' – by which she meant to shout louder, but later she realised that shouting was something she didn't have to do – enough feeling was there in her voice and a kind of simplicity, an avoidance of extremes, was inherent, and there in her best songs, effortless.

Her extravagant 'arias' were musically 'acting' – and she was never any good at that.

31

For example – in some songs she hardly seems to try; she lays her voice sleepily, dreamily, across the melody and the beat. It's completely relaxed and natural; she's not posing, not acting.

The colour of your eyes

No stranger am I

(These are more or less just different versions of the same musical idea)

Or, she just skips along against a jazzy backing; she makes it all sound so easy, the variation, the key changes.

Earthbound Gypsy

But of course she was trying; Dusty rarely sang a note that was not carefully thought out.

She did the art that conceals art; she liked the casual disposition of notes which of course was by no means casual.

32

Among the many of Dusty's legends is the one of her 'perfectionism', in recording and performance – it's a myth – at times a neurotic inability to stop fiddling around, to say something's finished and just leave it alone.

At other times it's simply a failure of care.

Some of your lovin': she pushes her voice along, times it nicely over the beat of the drumming and the muffled piano and it's a good tuneful rhythmic track – and then she spoils it all with a flubbed high note at the end. It's disconcerting, incongruous, jarring – like an intrusion from amateur night at the local pub. She knew it. She said: 'It's a really great song apart from one bum note which I contributed'.

And she knew that, and didn't re-record, didn't correct. She just let it go.

If you listen closely to Dusty's music you'll hear many surprisingly slipshod moments like this – times when *she'd done that* and *wasn't interested* anymore, *couldn't be bothered* and *perhaps no one would notice.*

There's a certain humanity in these small failings. In those days a few imperfections could be tolerated and maybe that's more like life, just life itself.

33

As a live artist, touring with her band ('my Echoes') and confident and easy with her fans and the surroundings of small clubs she might say to herself 'I'm not what you see' and it didn't matter – this was just one of the several spaces she inhabited and where she was comfortable.

Otherwise, for most of the 60s you'd find Dusty at home, really at home, at one place in the world: behind the bronze doors of Philips Studios near Marble Arch – and here, alone and together with her friends, her musicians, with Jonny Franz producing and the big machines recording, she lived in the songs she knew she could sing over and over again for as long as her patient commercial management allowed her to do so.

34

Dusty didn't apply the notion of 'concept' – otherwise known as 'theme or story'- to any of her albums, she didn't see them that way, and in practice they were often a sort of muddled dumping ground for songs she happened to like, and the nearest she ever came to providing a 'concept' was a landmark in her career and a confused piece of record making which turned out to be no one's concept.

Sooner or later we have to talk about ***Memphis***.

35

Dusty in Memphis was her supposed genuflection to US sound, soul, blues, whatever – to all those heroes she'd grown up listening to and admired, and from afar, copied.

She assumed, early on, a transatlantic accent in song because this was a necessary identification in pop and the way British pop singers with any ambition rid themselves of a parochial and therefore insignificant vocal tradition and instead pasted on to their output aspects of a blues derived culture while naturally owning nothing of that.

Dusty sang black derived songs and promoted Motown artists because this was music more interesting than the thin mild British Top 40 offerings around at the time; she loved the rhythm, the space those songs offered her vocal range, the history, the heritage: this was her New World.

But that was as far as it went. She never sounded 'black' or wished to; she was respectful of history and honest in that way and it was not, really, her type of singing. Her voice was not strong enough for traditional gospel or blues – and she always flourished best when she had a tune, written down for her, which was going somewhere. When she began she wanted to see the end.

So although Dusty did indeed go to Memphis she didn't record anything finished there – the main recording and the backing tracks, some of which she may never have heard once she'd done the vocals, were done at studios in New York. And what emerged from this smudged collaboration with Jerry Wexler (that neither knew much about each other was later abundantly clear) is an album of mixed tracks, mostly penned by white songwriters and rather insecurely placed musically which could just have well have been recorded in London.

So what was supposed to have been the definitive recording of her career received respectable if occasionally slightly baffled reviews and quickly disappeared.

Dusty herself, no doubt disappointed, had a realistic view: 'It's a good record but it's not a classic'.

The song she's now best known for, that turns up now and again on the radio, ***Son of a Preacher Man,*** is pretty much a pointless pastiche. She had no high regard for that kind of performance – 'it's a pretty white record'.

But it's still around because it's part of her myth: this British 'white soul singer'.

36

What went wrong in Memphis ?

Dusty, for all the mayhem of her personal life, preferred rules in music. At Philips many things were done for her and this allowed the right kind of freedom – within the rules.

In Tennessee she was asked, expected, to do things very differently and she couldn't adapt to the method and the mode – couldn't just go into the box and make it up, improvise, and she was also, fairly clearly, intimidated.

Everyone misunderstood each other. And some local musicians there, frankly, just didn't like her. Perhaps they sensed, and resented, without saying, that underlying her respect for the skills they possessed, she had a lifelong sense of entitlement.

This wasn't racial, it wasn't arrogance, it was more a combination of belief in herself, her gifts, and a class-based English sense of authority which she could possibly not have articulated but nevertheless conveyed.

And aspects of her private life became quickly known around Memphis and weren't welcomed.

This could not end well.

37

Years after Dusty was dead, and ***Dusty in Memphis*** had somehow slipped into that pantheon of 'albums you must hear before you die' a music critic described the recording, and her voice there, as *paramusical* , and *spacious,* and *somehow mysterious.*

And in straining to make sense of her music, its bewildering oscillation, the idea of *paramusical* is an idea as good as any to describe music beside music – without any meaning other than the aesthetic emotion.

The spaciousness and mystery resided in her voice - and there's a legend around her recording technique, how she sang to herself.

Sometimes she'd turn up the volume in her headphones so the backing track was acoustically invisible, unbearable, 'like singing into a void'.

She said she did this to help create an 'airy' sound.

So there was just her voice and nothing else.

38

Towards the end of Dusty's career in Britain, on the cusp of the sixties, and seventies, interviews she gave were already looking back –not self-consciously nostalgic but rather responding to the interviewers' determined perspective of *what had been* and not *what next ?*

Up in the north, on one of those tours which were so much part of her working life for years and paid money her records often failed to make, she talked to a journalist from one of the quality Sundays and while she answered questions she sewed repairs to her teddy bear Einstein, a toy acquired years before and part of her entourage – a long and durable relationship. Einstein travelled with her – he was faithful and he couldn't judge. There was a certain infantilism here – she had other toys, but it wasn't emphasised.

She worried, without saying so directly, about her future and ageing, and obsessed a bit over visible, but entirely natural, lines on her face. She was around thirty then.

A year or so later Ray Connelly at the *Evening Standard* chatted with her and wrote, among other things, 'I think Dusty's sad'. She said oh no, not at all, but the sadness which may have been apparent to others lay often unrevealed to herself and existed only in the plaintive grain of her music, which, by being so familiar, was beyond her rational understanding, or perception.

39

Read about the 70s now, or remember how it was then, and you'll realise how difficult things would have been for her in Britain.

Dusty talked, in various interviews and at various times, quite a lot about music, about songs and voice and performance, but she never saw pop music in a fashionable or cultural way. She didn't intellectualise or try to place herself in some kind of circle or be referential. She stayed aloof from changing musical trends. This was a certain wisdom – a recognition of the value of timelessness but her failure to retain an audience in her own country must have seemed harsh – a 'shame' she simply ran away from.

40

The panic she must have felt, as she saw her career sliding away, just leaving the residue of her earlier fame and security, the fans more or less stranded and no help to her – how easy it became to reach for all the things which were bad for her, laid out in a buffet of temptation, and nothing else, not even the music, left to sustain her.

In 1970 she recorded, in an unknown location, ***Morning Please Don't Come,*** a track hardly publicised and rarely heard – a song her brother Tom wrote for her and might have written just so she could sing as she sometimes did when she was young, alone or with the group, and she does that – her voice light and gently curling around the lyrics and Tom's own voice as he plays the guitar accompaniment barely audible, a little ghostly.

It's a song about loneliness, of course.

41

Dusty lived the 'romance' of life in the sixties, her voice and her look found its expression there, she was part of it – but then found herself on the sidelines and silent as time and fashion rolled by.

And Dusty didn't do TV like Cilla, not Cilla's later variety type shows where the role Cilla assumed was Cilla herself writ large, a genuine self, projected with integrity to a mass audience who recognised and appreciated that here there was no 'act'.

Dusty couldn't do that – she couldn't 'act' and she couldn't be herself. She later claimed this was somehow down to 'shyness' but it's more likely the shyness was self-consciousness mixed with a certain *de haut en bas*, a lack of common touch which, live, often translated into a breathless nerviness in performance. It's alienating – and perhaps picked up an essential uncomfortable truth about herself: she succeeded as a recording artist because that's what she preferred to be. She was not open to the public eye.

So in later years that television option, a possible new path away from her failing career, was closed to her.

42

In 1972, against much good advice, Dusty packed up her sequinned dresses, said goodbye to her band and moved to the US. And then it was as if you had opened a trapdoor in her world and she tripped and just fell and fell.

43

To realise the extent of the *dégringolade,* to understand what happened to her in California, you'd have to have known the people she mixed with and the values – short sighted, materialistic, fantasising, *benignly corrupt* in fact, that welcomed her, enfolded her and then failed her.

Offered a home and a future she found neither.

The milieu she inhabited did not inculcate in her any sense of realism and did not allow her, even at 31 or so, to grow, to develop a worthy sense of self.

So she moved from bar to bar and from bed to bed and in and out of this or that recording studio. She went on singing because that was her life, what she'd always done and she eventually fashioned a style to suit her diminished vocal range but the sound (we're not at Philips anymore) became mannered and affected, the tracks were mediocre and the music was gone.

And like many a fading star before her Dusty became, famewise, posthumous in her own life.

As for regrets – she may not have had those, she moved through the world very much in the present – and in any case she no longer had the voice or was offered the material through which to express those regrets artistically.

44

You might also guess that in the United States her potential audience couldn't understand her because her musical terminology wasn't theirs. Her vocal sadness didn't translate into a meaning American listeners could embrace, identify with, because it didn't seem related to an experience of real, historic, suffering – not black, not poor, not poor and black or poor and white. The sadness was in her timbre and inherent and floated free of specific social or cultural burdens and therefore existed in the margins.

45

There's not much more to say about Dusty, musically.

While she was away, or even earlier, pop music began to turn in different directions.

The lone voice began to lose authority.

She'd grown up in a time when the individual voice, unaided by sophisticated electronics, was supreme.

The best thing to do is listen to those songs where her voice, framed on the four track recording of her heyday, delivers just that:

I can't give back the love I feel for you

It's one of her favourite songs, full of the musical changes she did so well.

But it wasn't remotely commercial.

46

She knew how good she was, how could she not, but she may not have recognised that as she moved quixotically and often magically through musical styles she became alone, isolated and opaque to new generations.

Past a popular performer's heyday there must be consistent and enduring strands that pull a reputation through into a new contemporary time and place – perpetually in the present.

That didn't happen with Dusty – the strands were severed, disconnected, sometimes her work was wonderful *but who'd listen to it ?*

And then aspects of her music, not so much the music itself, was taken up again, hijacked you could say, to support identities which have no real relation to her career and be exploited by whoever needs to become attached to them.

46

Too often Dusty littered with broken hearts the places she left behind.

She never felt she had to explain about anything; she wanted people to accept her the way she was – she'd be around and then she'd be gone, moved on, and that would be that.

And in spite of her faithlessness, which was chronic with her, perhaps someone or other might cherish the time they'd had.

About her personal life there were plenty of stories circulating clandestinely and she probably found some of those funny as long as they stayed secret.

She may even have found an attractive drama in duplicity – she wasn't cruel so much as liking to be the centre of things and enjoying a kind of humour in the game of hiding.

47

There is something known in the business world as a *corporate veil.*

Philips flung corporate veils over Dusty.

The corporate veil was protection; her teasing character occasionally peeped around the veil – she may have experienced longings to pierce it from time to time but she had a justified fear of doing so.

She'd grown up in an era where secrecy was paramount but really it was in her nature and she maintained that stance all her life. Long into the years where openness wouldn't have mattered and attitudes had changed she never publicly identified herself as gay or publicly supported gay causes – she would have seen personal reticence as her right and of no relevance to her music.

48

Sometime at the end of the 70s, in one of Dusty's journeys back to England, her fan club member Sharon Davies discussed writing a biography.

'I'd like to read it,' was the response – as if by that time her own life was closed and a part of history, external to her, a 'legend' to be read from outside herself, and then, and only then, to be rendered comprehensible.

And 'be kind', she said.

A Girl Called Dusty was published nearly twenty years later. There's nothing in it she could have really objected to (from beyond the grave) but you suspect, on a casual flip through, that there's not much she would have found very interesting either. It's a generous interpretation – a pleasant ramble along well worn paths – a fan's book, in the best sense.

The title has its own significance, its own irony. From a certain perspective Dusty never ceased being a 'girl' – trapped in the amber of her reputation in the sixties, in the days when you could go on being a girl for a long time because 'woman' meant something rather different: the idea of maturity, settling down, growing up sexually – yesterday's themes. In practice something from those themes might have helped her but in the course of events she never got around to them.

49

When she was starting out on her career, experimenting with her voice and with the people she would be singing with, crafting her music with, she was in such a hurry, so keen to be known, that she didn't have time to do the step by step growing that develops naturally in most of us – and then, when the days came when it was necessary to behave in a different way, a better way, to cope with whatever life hands you – well, she couldn't do that.

50

Dusty was a narcissist, in common with many performers, since performing is an unnatural act, and she was also a masochist. The origins of her wish to be hurt are a mystery, but she sought and often found, physical pain and physical damage.

There's no evidence, in spite of these aberrations, that she ever wanted to look too deeply into her own mind – she tended to avoid analysis and would have completely despised 'psychobiography'.

You're left with a conundrum - with the sometimes self-defeating oddness of her life in music, the lack of connections, the obdurate persistence in pursuing a musical catalogue which, for a popular singer, really did not work.

She seemed to exist outside consciousness in that way.

But there isn't anything clear – Dusty was the least autobiographical of singers. You couldn't see her using those confessional songs of the singer-songwriters in the seventies as reaching out to an audience, giving some kind of explanation.

She sang some of those songs, but only as performance.

51

So she became a bit of a tattered diva, an idol to a lot of people who really knew nothing about her music, remembered nothing about her prime.

It's sad – what's often written about her – the focus of attention on her sexuality – what couldn't matter less.

The books, the shows, they're nothing. She's not there.

She tried as hard as she could; she stayed as long as she could. She may have wanted things to be different; she may have wanted stability in relationships and to find new and different modes of popular music expression but her temperament denied her the one and changing times and the diminishment of her voice, the other.

Dusty left no musical heritage; like Billie Holiday, who resembles Dusty only in the arc of their different careers, she has no heirs and no one could ever possibly learn from her.

She was a genius, in a way.

'I'm tired of being a pop singer,' she said, in a moment of true, if psychologically self-destructive, insight.

It's the most profound comment she ever made about her profession, her life, and the end it all came to.

52

Mary O'Brien found it easy to assume *Dusty Springfield's* identity. To her it was a natural expression of difference – a drama attached to her career, a necessary mask. There was no disruption of personality – the duality existed as a natural part of her story.

At the end of her life she famously said: 'I just want to die as Mary O'Brien.'

Also known as.

She saw no confusion. She'd always known who she was.

And that's how her death certificate was written.

53

When the time came for her to die, she was, at least outwardly, stoical and a bit fatalistic. Possibly she understood and accepted, the lapsed Catholic, a kind of spiritual pattern to her life and career – through early success then a kind of dissipation and then, after her return to England, final redemption.

In her youth she could stand still for nothing but in her last days she wanted peace and she died in peace by the old river.

'Sweet Thames run softly till I end my song'

A Medley

(in every sense of the word)

Far Way Places
Recorded 30 January 1962
Philips Studios Stanhope Place

Island of Dreams
Recorded 15 October 1962
Philips Studios Stanhope Place

Silver Threads and Golden Needles
Recorded April 1962
Philips Studios Stanhope Place

No Sad Songs for Me
Recorded 1963
Philips Studios Stanhope Place

Where Have All The Flowers Gone ?
(sung in German)
Recorded 6 March 1963
Olympic Sound Studios London
(all with The Springfields)

Don't Say it Baby
Recorded September 1964
New York

I've Been Wrong Before
Recorded 15 June 1965
Philips Studios Stanhope Place

That's How Heartaches Are Made
Recorded 2 July 1965
Philips Studios Stanhope Place

Take Me For a While
Recorded 26 November 1965
Philips Studios Stanhope Place

If It Hadn't Been For You
Recorded 30 December 1965
Philips Studios Stanhope Place

I'm Gonna Leave You
Recorded 15 June 1966
Philips Studios Stanhope Place

Poor Wayfaring Stranger
September 1 1966
Live BBC TV

No Stranger Am I
Recorded 27 July 1967
Philips Studios Stanhope Place

Chained to A Memory
Recorded 10 August 1967
Philips Studios Stanhope Place

Time After Time
Recorded 8 August 1967
Philips Studios Stanhope Place

Spooky
Recorded 24 January 1968
Philips Studios Stanhope Place

It's Over
Recorded March 1968
Philips Studios Stanhope Place

In The Land Of Make Believe
Recorded September 1968
Vocals recorded in New York

The Colour of Your Eyes
Recorded 23 August 1968
Olympic Studios London

Mr Dream Merchant
Recorded August 1968
Philips Studios Stanhope Place

I Only Wanna Laugh
Recorded 7 August 1968
Philips Studios Stanhope Place

I' Can't Give Back The Love I Feel For You
Recorded 23 October 1968
Olympic Studios London

Who Will Take My Place ?
Recorded 22 November 1968
Philips Studios Stanhope Place

Second Time Around
Recorded 22 November 1968
Philips Studios Stanhope Place

Morning Please Don't Come
Recorded 22 April 1969
Recording site unknown

Am I The Same Girl ?
Recorded August 1969
Philips Studios Stanhope Place

Earthbound Gypsy
Recorded 1969
Philips Studios Stanhope Place

A Brand New Me
Recorded 5 October 1969
Sigma Sound Studios Philadelphia

Never Love Again
Recorded 21 September 1969
Sigma Sound Studios Philadelphia

Joe
Recorded October 1969
Sigma Sound Studios Philadelphia

Wasn't Born To Follow
Recorded June 1970
Trident Studios/Philips Studios London

You've Got a Friend
Recorded 1971
Century Sound Studios New York

(Recording details from The Complete Dusty Springfield Ed Paul Howes, London 2001)

Printed in Great Britain
by Amazon